Crime and punishment in c.1000–present

Crime and punishment in medieval England: c.1000–c.1500

The Anglo-Saxon period

1. If someone was murdered, what type of system might be used to settle the matter and ensure the murderer was punished?

....

....

2. Who was in charge of law and order in a settlement?

....

....

3. What was the most common 'type' of crime?

....

....

4. How did Anglo-Saxon communities ensure a criminal on the run was caught?

....

....

5. As well as trial by jury, what other type of 'trial' (often conducted by the Church) was used in this period?

....

....

6. What was the 'wergild'?

....

....

7. At what age were men expected to become part of the system of law and order? And what was this system called?

....

....

....

8 Which people in society had their rights and property most protected by the law?

....

....

9 Why did few people in society regard poaching as a crime?

....

....

10 Define each of the following three 'types' of crime and give two examples of each.

	Crimes against the person	Crimes against property	Crimes against authority
Definition			
Example 1			
Example 2			

The Norman period

11 Put these events in chronological order by writing one of the numbers 1–4 in the empty column, with 1 being the earliest and 4 the latest. If you want to challenge yourself further, you could also include the dates of these events.

Event	Chronological order (1–4)	Do I know the date?
Henry II ensured laws were written down. This helped to create standard laws across the country for the first time.		
William I introduced new murdrum laws, the Forest Laws and ended the payment of the wergild. The Normans also introduced Church courts (to be used for trying churchmen).		
William of Normandy became the King of England and needed to introduce laws that would help him to exert his power and control.		
The Anglo-Saxon kings had started to issue 'codes' that protected their own property and interests.		

Change and continuity in law enforcement and punishment

12 In the essay questions, you may be asked to evaluate a statement about the past, meaning that you will need to consider the arguments for and against. The statements below are not full exam questions but will help you to consider potential essays. Look at the statements below and try to think of a couple of reasons in support of, and against, each one.

a 'By the end of the medieval period, law enforcement and punishment had changed very little since 1100.'

Arguments for	Arguments against

b 'Key parts of law enforcement and punishment had remained the same since 1100. However, trials and policing methods had improved.'

Arguments for	Arguments against

c 'By the end of the Middle Ages law enforcement and punishment had almost totally changed. They were unrecognisable.'

Arguments for	Arguments against

d Which of the statements a–c is the most correct? Explain your argument in the space below. It may help you to include some of the terms from the following box.

tithings	hue and cry	clergy	poaching
ordeal	social	Forest Laws	court
nobles	the Church	stocks	property
treason	sheriff	constable	sanctuary
murdrum	corporal	community	fines
jury	combat	person	king
capital	hundred	peasantry	

....

....

....

....

....

Case study
The Church's role in law and order in the medieval period

13 Read each statement and decide whether it is true or false. Correct the false statements in the space provided below.

Statement	True/False
William I introduced Church courts during his reign (1066–87).	True/False
There was no tension at all between the Church and the king's authority.	True/False
The argument between Thomas Becket and Henry II indicated that there was tension over how the Church courts treated criminals.	True/False
Henry II thought that his own royal courts should have been the most powerful in the land.	True/False
Church courts often sentenced people to death.	True/False
Only priests could be tried in the Church courts.	True/False
Sanctuary meant that someone on the run could avoid being arrested.	True/False
Trial by ordeal was believed to be a fair way of deciding on someone's guilt or innocence if a jury could not decide.	True/False
Pope Innocent III ended trial by ordeal in 1315.	True/False

....

....

....

....

....

....

Exam-style questions

14 Explain one way in which types of law enforcement were different under the Anglo-Saxons and later medieval periods.

⏱ 6   **4 marks**

....

....

....

....

....

....

....

....

15 Explain why there was disagreement over the role of Church courts in the later medieval period.

You may use the following in your answer:

■ trial by ordeal
■ benefit of clergy

You **must** also use information of your own. If you run out of space, you may continue your answer on a separate piece of paper.

⏱ 18   **12 marks**

....

....

....

....

....

....

....

....

....

....

....

....

....

....

....

16 'The main purpose of law making during the medieval period was to protect the property of the king.' How far do you agree? Explain your answer.

You may use the following in your answer:

- Forest Laws
- stocks and pillories

You **must** also use information of your own. If you run out of space, you may continue your answer on a separate piece of paper.

24 **16 marks**

....

....

....

....

....

....

....

....

....

....

....

....

....

....

....

....

....

....

....

....

....

....

Crime and punishment in early modern England: c.1500–c.1700

Changes to society and crimes between c.1500 and c.1700

17 Circle or highlight the correct answer(s). Each question states the number to look for.

a During the medieval period, which two institutions/groups were the most powerful in society?

the Church	hundred	tithing	the monarchy

b What happened to the population during the sixteenth and seventeenth centuries? (There are two correct answers.)

There was a steady increase in the population.	Unemployment grew.	People remained living in rural communities.	There was a rapid increase in the population.

c Which one statement best describes what was happening to England's economy during the period c.1500–c.1700?

A small group of people got richer.	Some people got richer but many people remained poor, and vulnerable to price rises or unemployment.	Bad harvests and disrupted trade affected many in the population.	Overall, England became wealthier.

d Which one event was a key development for the sharing of information during the period c.1500–c.1700?

The publication of an English Bible	The Reformation	The invention of the printing press	The English Civil War

e Which Tudor monarch began making changes within the English Church? (There is one correct answer.)

Henry VIII	Edward VI	Mary I	Elizabeth I

f As a result of religious changes and disagreements in this period, which two crimes became more common?

poaching	heresy	vagabondage	treason

g What impact did the English Civil War have on the population? (Choose one statement that best describes the impact.)

Many in the country felt like 'the world turn'd upside down' and there was increased instability.	The country was more united under Oliver Cromwell and could start to introduce Puritan law.	Many people were displaced and so went back to their rural communities.	Charles I's execution resolved the religious disputes.

h What happened to protect landowners' rights during this period? (There is one correct answer.)

The number of poachers fell.	Land was enclosed and was used by the landowner only.	Many people moved to towns and cities.	Poaching laws were strengthened.

18 From the 1500s onwards people increasingly feared the 'new' crimes of vagabondage and witchcraft. Fill in the table in order to test your knowledge of these crimes (several examples have been completed for you).

	Vagabondage and vagrancy	Witchcraft
Write *one* definition of this crime:	This is the crime of being a wandering beggar.	
Give *two* reasons why this was regarded as a crime in the early modern period:		It went against church teachings and was seen as 'heresy'.
State *three* facts you can remember about this type of crime:		Many pamphlets were produced that had witchcraft as their topic.
Write down *four* ways that these criminals could be treated/ punished by society:	Some vagrants were whipped.	
In no more than *five* lines, explain why this crime was seen as a threat during the early modern period:	It was believed that harsh treatment would discourage...	

19 Write a few lines to explain each of the trends below. The correct answers from Question 17 in this section might help you.

a   The increase in crime during the 1500s and early 1600s happened because...

....

....

....

b   There was an increased fear of crime during the period c.1500–c.1700 because...

....

....

....

c   Tougher laws surrounding crimes against property were created in the early modern period because...

....

....

....

d There were also tougher laws surrounding crimes against royal and Church authority because...

....

....

....

....

e There was an increase in the use of capital punishment from the 1680s because...

....

....

....

....

Law enforcement and punishment in the early modern period

20 For each type of law enforcement or punishment listed below, you should indicate 'remained' (from the medieval period) or 'changed' (this was introduced, or altered, in the period c.1500–c.1700). If you decide something changed during this period, use a separate piece of paper to write a line to explain how it changed/what it changed to.

Example:

	Remained	Changed
Justices of the Peace dealt with minor crimes and local rules.		Y

This is a change because Justices of the Peace were more organised than the medieval courts and system like the 'hue and cry'.

Who dealt with crimes?		
	Remained	Changed
Quarter sessions were held four times a year and JPs would make judgements.		
County Assizes were held twice yearly, which allowed royal judges to deal with more serious crimes.		
Tithings and the hue and cry system were used in smaller communities.		
Watchmen and sergeants were found in towns.		
The Church was very involved in making decisions on some crimes (e.g. heresy).		
Witchcraft could now be tried in ordinary courts.		
Parish constables were employed.		
Citizens who had been robbed were expected to locate and catch the criminal.		
Benefit of the clergy still existed, apart from the most serious crimes.		
The Habeas Corpus law meant that people had to be tried within a certain time frame.		
The army was occasionally used to deal with riots, unrest or criminals.		

What types of punishments were used?		
	Remained	Changed
Vagabonds could be flogged and sent back to where they came from.		
Stocks were used for those who could not pay fines.		
Pillories were commonly employed for offences like underselling goods or cheating in a game of cards.		
Debtors could be put in prison.		
Corporal and capital punishment were both used.		
Houses of Correction were built in every county (beggars were sent there).		
The Bloody Code outlined many crimes (minor and major) that could be punishable by death.		
Transportation was used for serious criminals who had avoided the death penalty.		

What attempts were made to prevent crime?		
	Remained	Changed
The pillories were used to embarrass and make an example of those who had committed minor crimes.		
Executions were public — this was a good way of making an example of criminals.		
'Poor rates' were introduced in certain parishes to try and prevent poor people within the parish becoming vagrants, or committing crimes out of necessity.		
The punishments for certain crimes were made deliberately harsh to dissuade people from committing them.		
Pamphlets were produced to warn people about crime and possible punishments.		

Case studies

What can the cases of the Gunpowder Plot (1605) and Matthew Hopkins (1645–47) tell us about early modern crime, law and order?

21 **Read the accounts below and use what you already know about each case study to answer the questions alongside each account.**

a

Religion under James I was complicated. There were many divisions that remained from the Reformation and between the different religious groups in society. Some plotters moved to get rid of the king, including Robert Catesby and Guy Fawkes. This would involve storing gunpowder under the Houses of Parliament and using it to kill the king. However the plot was discovered. After being caught, the plotters were tortured, and hung, drawn and quartered in London.	What were the reasons for the plot?
	What were the authorities concerned about?
	What message did the punishment of the plotters send out?

b

In 1645, Matthew Hopkins and his assistant John Stearne began to search East Anglia for witches. Hopkins named 36 women as witches and collected 'evidence' of them using harmful magic. Many of the women were old or poor. Hopkins questioned the suspects while keeping them awake, standing or moving, and by watching carefully to see whether symbols of the Devil, like animals or insects, entered the room. Further 'proof' was gathered by checking the suspects' bodies for 'Devil's marks', such as boils, scars or spots. Towns and villages across East Anglia began inviting Hopkins to help them find witches. He often charged for his services. The local vicar at Brandeston was accused of witchcraft and 'swum' to see if he was guilty. Marks were found in his mouth and he was hanged. Hopkins seemed to stop working around 1647, but the period 1645–47 saw at least 100 executions for witchcraft in East Anglia.	What were the reasons for the witch-hunt?
	What were Hopkins and others concerned about?
	What message did the trial and punishment of those accused of witchcraft send out?

Exam-style questions

22 **Explain one way in which types of punishment were similar during the medieval and early modern periods.**

⏱ 6   **4 marks**

....

....

....

....

....

....

....

....

23 Why did the use of the Bloody Code increase during the period c.1500–c.1700?

You may use the following in your answer:

- transportation
- population growth

You **must** also use information of your own. If you run out of space, you may continue your answer on a separate piece of paper.

(18) (12 marks)

Why did the use of the Bloody Code increase during the period c.1500–c.1700?

You may use the following in your answer:

24 'Religion was the most important factor influencing how criminal activity was dealt with during the period c.1000–c.1700.' How far do you agree? Explain your answer.

You may use the following in your answer:

- laws against witchcraft
- benefit of the clergy

You **must** also use information of your own. If you run out of space, you may continue your answer on a separate piece of paper.

24 **16 marks**

Crime and punishment in eighteenth- and nineteenth-century Britain: c.1700–c.1900
Nature and changing definitions of criminal activity

25 Go through each type of crime in the table and tick the boxes that apply. An example has been completed for you.

Type of criminal activity	Commonly found in towns	Commonly happened in the country	Likely to affect ordinary people	Likely to affect the landowning classes	Could make money for the person doing it	Could disrupt trade	Punishment was severe
Pickpocketing and petty theft	✓		✓	✓	✓		✓
Smuggling							
Industrial action/trade unionism							
Poaching							
Highway robbery							
Selling on the black market							

26 Using the following terms, and the information in the table in Question 25, fill in the blanks in the paragraph below. Be careful: there are three obvious mistakes that need to be corrected.

employment	Black Act	witchcraft
professional	duties	violent
industrial	community	better
petty theft	landowning	transported
coastal		

Between 1700 and 1900 towns grew in size. This was often due to the presence of more

.... in the new factories found in .... towns. There

were consequences — a larger urban population, fewer people who knew each other that

well and the sense of .... decreased somewhat. Because more people

crowded together, it was easier to commit and get away with a crime. In this kind of

setting, ... gangs of thieves and criminals could operate. Poverty became

more common and some had to commit crimes just to survive — by stealing food or

.... (to sell on goods that they pickpocketed), for example.

As Britain grew wealthy from trade and a larger .... class developed,

property was more of a concern for the authorities. Travellers feared highway robberies,

especially on some of the main routes into Liverpool. Highwaymen could be ruthless and

....

Poaching had long existed. After the .... of 1723, poaching became punishable by death — which shows how much the landowners and authorities were worried about it; even if communities thought these types of laws were very **fair**. Smuggling (especially in .... areas) meant that the government lost out on taxes and .... The Bloody Code said that smuggling was a **minor** crime but it still continued.

Finally, another big change in what was thought of as criminal activity related to the new trade unions, rather than 'old' crimes like .... When groups such as the Tolpuddle Martyrs tried to work together for .... rights, employers and the government regarded them as dangerous. These unfortunate men were arrested and .... to Australia in 1833.

The nature of law enforcement and punishment during c.1700–c.1900

27 Put these events, which show changes in how the law was enforced, in chronological order by writing one of the numbers 1–13 in the empty column, with 1 being the earliest and 13 the latest. If you want to challenge yourself further, you could also include the dates of these events.

Event	Chronological order (1–13)	Do I know the date?
Police helmets were introduced.		
The Metropolitan Police Force was set up in London.		
The Bow Street Runners established a new patrol of 54 men.		
A new law was passed allowing all counties to set up their own police forces.		
There were 200+ police forces and 39,000 police officers across Britain.		
A new law was passed allowing all towns to set up their own police forces.		
The Metropolitan Police Force set up a criminal investigation department (CID), which was soon copied across the country.		
Large-scale protests in Britain meant some were scared of revolution.		
It became compulsory for all towns and counties to have a police force.		
Robert Peel was appointed as home secretary.		
Watchmen and parish constables led the community in patrolling the streets and catching criminals.		
The Metropolitan Police Force set up the first detective force.		
The Bow Street Runners were established in London.		

28 For each type of punishment, think about what changed in the period c.1700–c.1900, and then fill in the 'later' column.

Punishment	Earlier in the period...	Later in the period...
The Bloody Code	This meant that many crimes were punishable by death. In 1765, the number was 160 and by 1815 this had risen to 225, including crimes such as poaching or cutting down trees.	
Transportation	This was seen as a punishment that would make juries willing to convict, as it was not as harsh as death but still an excellent deterrent. Convicts were sent to America in the 1600s and Australia, once the USA became independent.	
Prisons	Prisons were generally seen as a place for criminals awaiting trial or those in debt (60% of inmates in 1777). There was little separation of the different types of inmates, meaning the system was seen as a 'school for crime'.	

29 Can you add an explanation as to why each change happened?

Type of punishment	Why it changed
The Bloody Code	It changed because...
Transportation	
Prisons	

Case studies

What was Pentonville Prison like?

30 Read each statement and decide whether it is true or false. Correct the false statements in the space provided below.

Statement	True/False
In the mid-1800s the government built a large number of new prisons in Britain.	True/False
Pentonville was built to hold petty criminals arrested for crimes such as pickpocketing.	True/False
Pentonville was a holding prison for those awaiting transportation or the death penalty.	True/False
Each block of Pentonville was built like a spoke of a wheel, so that the guards could see each wing from the centre. As such, fewer guards were required to patrol the prison.	True/False
Inmates at Pentonville were allowed to be freely in contact with one another.	True/False
Prisoners at Pentonville were exposed to Christian principles such as hard work.	True/False

....

....

....

....

....

How successful was the separate system?

31 The following statements relate to the separate system. Fill out the table below, deciding whether each statement is a strength or weakness of the system.

- The separate system stopped prisoners mixing with each other and sharing criminal ideas.
- Solitary confinement could be damaging for a prisoner's mental health.
- Prisoners were trained in work, such as how to use a loom, so were able to seek employment upon release.
- The system was costly to build and run because the prisoners needed to be kept separate.

Strengths	Weaknesses

Exam-style questions

32 Explain one way in which types of punishment in the early modern period were different to those of the eighteenth and nineteenth centuries.

⏱ 6 · **4 marks**

....

....

....

....

....

....

....

33 Explain why there were changes to the organisation of law enforcement during the period c.1700–c.1900.

You may use the following in your answer:

- Robert Peel
- the Bow Street Runners

You **must** also use information of your own. If you run out of space, you may continue your answer on a separate piece of paper.

⏱ 18 · **12 marks**

....

....

....

....

....

....

....

....

....

....

....

....

....

....

34 'The main purpose of punishment during the period c.1700–c.1900 was to deter people from committing crimes.' How far do you agree? Explain your answer.

You may use the following in your answer:

- the ending of transportation
- Pentonville Prison

You **must** also use information of your own. If you run out of space, you may continue your answer on a separate piece of paper.

24 **16 marks**

....
....
....
....
....
....
....
....
....
....
....
....
....
....
....
....
....
....
....
....
....
....

'The main purpose of punishment during the period c.1700–c.1900 was to deter people from committing crimes.' How far do you agree? Explain your answer.

Crime and punishment in modern Britain: c.1900–present
Nature and changing definitions of criminal activity in the twentieth century

35 There were many changes that took place in the twentieth century that led to differences in the way crimes were committed, categorised and recorded. Place the following changes in order in the table below. Which do you think had the largest impact and why? An example has been completed for you.

Creation of the welfare state	Police are better trained	New technologies	Multiculturalism	Many people are wealthier

Rank	Change in the twentieth century	What impact has this had, and why?
1 (example)	New technologies	Technologies (such as the car) have increased types of crime (cars can be stolen, insurance fraud etc.). Computers and the internet have created the opportunity for many more types of crime, such as cyber-crime.
2		
3		
4		
5		

36 Sort the following types of crime into the three categories in the table below.

Speeding	Hate crime	Murder
Terrorism	Rape	Theft
Shoplifting	Car theft	Online fraud
Drug smuggling	Modern-day slavery	Vandalism

Category	Crime/s
Crimes that had existed previously	
Old crimes in a new form	
'New' crime	

The nature of law enforcement and punishment in the twentieth century

37 There are six mistakes in the following paragraph. Circle them and then rewrite the paragraph with corrections in the space provided below (if you run out of space, continue on a separate piece of paper).

> The police force across the UK has decreased in size since the 1800s, which is the first way that crime is prevented — fewer officers means more capacity. In addition to this, crime prevention officers (CPOs) were introduced in order to advise the population on things like security, for example alarms on property and vehicles. These officers have exactly the same powers as police officers. Since the mid-1900s, the police have supported Neighbourhood Watch groups in their efforts to report suspicious activities for the community to follow up and investigate. There is less attention given to young offenders, as it is thought that this will encourage them to turn to crime.

38 The police force modernised greatly in the twentieth century. In the following table tick the categories that apply to each change in the police force. An example has been completed for you.

Change in the police force	New technology	Better training and organisation	Funding and resources	Working with the community
Use of weapons (pepper spray, CS gas)	✓		✓	
Specialist units (firearms, drug squads)				
Standardised basic training				
Closed-circuit television (CCTV)				
Automatic Number Plate Recognition (ANPR)				
Two-way radios				
Community activities (crowd control, missing persons)				
Increased size of police force				
Use of computer technology/records				
Scientific investigation (e.g. DNA samples)				
Police vehicles and transport				
Community liaison officers (CPOs, officers in schools)				

39 There are a number of short-answer questions below. For each, decide which is the correct answer from the two statements supplied and circle or highlight it.

Short-answer question	Statement 1	Statement 2
What were the biggest changes to the prison system in the early part of the twentieth century?	There were no big changes — prisons remained much the same as they had done in Victorian times (e.g. solitary confinement and hard labour).	Things became less harsh in prisons — solitary confinement was ended after 1922 and living conditions were greatly improved.
Why were open prisons introduced after 1933?	They were cheaper.	Many believed that they would gradually prepare prisoners for a reintroduction to society.
How did attitudes about prisoners change in the twentieth century?	The public were more concerned about big events, such as the two world wars.	People feared crime and criminals less than in the Victorian era, and there was a greater belief in the benefits of education and rehabilitation.
Why did prisoner numbers increase after the Second World War?	The population of Britain increased, so there were proportionally more criminals.	More crimes were reported and prosecuted and carried longer prison sentences. There were also more people on remand.
What challenges faced the prison service in the late twentieth century to today?	Challenges included budgets, staffing, prisoner safety and prison living conditions.	Challenges included a lack of support from the general population and governments regarding the importance of prisons.

40 Sort the following statements relating to the treatment of young offenders into the two opposing columns in the table below.

- From 1903 onwards, borstals and approved schools were opened, which indicated there was a willingness to treat young people differently to adults who had offended.
- Since 1948, attendance centres have tried to educate young offenders, through teaching them life skills and offering them the chance to think about the impact of their offence(s) on the community.
- Borstals and youth detention centres have not reduced rates of re-offending.
- Young offenders who have had custodial sentences (have been detained) have the highest chance of re-offending.
- Increasingly, the authorities have recognised that they need to think carefully about the young offender's life as a whole — there have been increased efforts to include schools, social workers and parents.
- Blame does not always fall on the young person — sometimes parents can be fined, or young people removed from their care.
- There are several stages before a young person goes to a young offenders institution (YOI), such as working with them in education, at home and at attendance centres.
- YOIs can be quite similar to prisons.
- Other methods of monitoring young offenders, like tagging and curfews, are commonly used.

Things have improved for young offenders	Things have not improved/stayed the same for young offenders

41 For each type of non-custodial alternative to prison listed in the following table, try to think of the arguments both for and against it. An example has been completed for you.

Non-custodial punishment	Argument(s) for	Argument(s) against
Electronic tagging and curfews	Allows earlier release from prison/ suspended sentences Authorities can keep a constant watch on the offender's whereabouts	Technology — cost? Not a great deterrent to some
Probation and probation officers		
Fines		
Parole and suspended sentences		
Community service		

42 Read the statement below. It is similar to the type of statement you may see in an essay on this exam paper. How far do you agree with the statement? Write a short paragraph that outlines your argument.

'Changes to forms of punishment in the twentieth century show that there was a greater concern for rehabilitation of the criminal.'

....

....

....

....

....

Case studies

The treatment of conscientious objectors in the First and Second World Wars

43 **Use your knowledge of this topic to answer each of the questions below.**

a   Why were conscientious objectors viewed 'criminally' and as problems by society during the two world wars?

....

....

....

....

....

....

b   How were conscientious objectors treated in the First World War?

....

....

....

....

....

....

c   How were conscientious objectors treated in the Second World War?

....

....

....

....

....

....

d   What changed for conscientious objectors between the two world wars? What remained the same?

....

....

....

....

....

....

Derek Bentley and the abolition of the death penalty

44 Use your knowledge of this topic to include as much specific factual information as you can in each of the spaces below.

The evidence against Derek Bentley	Flaws in the evidence against Derek Bentley
Why were people concerned about the way Derek Bentley was treated?	**How does the case of Derek Bentley show how public attitudes towards the death penalty had changed?**

45 The death penalty was abolished in 1965. Create a spider diagram and try to suggest as many reasons as possible as to why it was abolished.

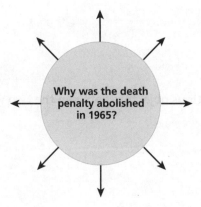

Why was the death penalty abolished in 1965?

Exam-style questions

46 Explain one way in which policing was different in the 1800s to the 1900s.

⏱ 6   **4 marks**

....

....

....

....

....

47 Explain why there were changes in the treatment of young offenders in the twentieth century.

You may use the following in your answer:

■ borstals
■ non-custodial sentences

You **must** also use information of your own. If you run out of space, you may continue your answer on a separate piece of paper.

⏱ 18   **12 marks**

....

....

....

....

....

....

....

....

....

....

....

....

....

....

....

....

....

48 'The introduction of many new technologies in the twentieth century greatly changed criminal activities and law enforcement.' How far do you agree? Explain your answer.

You may use the following in your answer:

- computers
- smuggling

You **must** also use information of your own. If you run out of space, you may continue your answer on a separate piece of paper.

(24) **16 marks**

....

....

....

....

....

....

....

....

....

....

....

....

....

....

....

....

....

....

....

....

....

The historic environment: Whitechapel, c.1870–c.1900

Whitechapel, c.1870–c.1900: crime, policing and the inner city, and the knowledge, selection and use of sources for historical enquiries

The area of Whitechapel

1 Circle or highlight the correct answer(s) for each question.

a   What were the very poorest parts of Whitechapel known as?

slums	rookeries	workhouses	beats

b   Which place was **not** a well-known location in Whitechapel?

Ten Bells Pub	Flower and Dean Street	Peabody Estate	Square Mile

c   What were the temporary lodgings that people could pay for by the night called?

tenancies	doss houses	lodgings	tenements

d   What colour were the areas on Booth's map where 'vicious, semi-criminal' inhabitants were said to live?

black	blue	red	pink

e   What was typical of conditions in the workhouses?

Inmates were expected to work hard (e.g. picking oakum).	Families were kept together.	Male and female inmates were segregated.	Food rations were minimal.

f   What was the name of the hospital which served the Whitechapel area?

The Royal Bethlehem	The Royal London	The Whitechapel Mission	St Bartholomew's Hospital

g   Which of the following areas was **not** close to Whitechapel?

Spitalfields	Bethnal Green	Wapping	Westminster

2 What types of source might be useful for finding out more about the area of Whitechapel? An example has been completed for you.

Type of source	Useful or not?	How could it be useful/what could it tell us? or What doesn't it tell us and what could I use instead?
Local newspapers	Useful	Because it is local and gives more information about the area itself. The source is likely to focus on specific stories/events to do with that area and give detail about the people of the area.
Census reports		
Old Bailey court reports		
National newspapers		
Local police reports from bobbies on the 'beat'		

The population in Whitechapel

3 Using the following terms, fill in the blanks in the paragraph below.

political	Workers' Friend	docks	anarchism
isolated	sweatshops	Fenians	multicultural

Whitechapel in the late 1800s was a busy and industrious area. Inhabitants might work

in the ...., tanneries or even .... The local area was crowded

and very ...., with immigrants from across Europe, including Russians,

Irish and Jews. The latter group would often settle in the same area and remain quite

.... There were concerns over some of the .... beliefs of

Whitechapel residents, for example there were supporters of socialism, communism and

.... , as well as Irish nationalists, who were known as .... A

political paper, the .... , was published in the Berners Street Theatre.

4 What types of source might be useful for finding out more about the population of Whitechapel? An example has been completed for you.

Type of source	Useful or not?	How could it be useful/what could it tell us? or What doesn't it tell us and what could I use instead?
Coroners' reports	Not	These would focus specifically on one person and their death. They would record basic details about that person but are unlikely to say much about how the person came to be in Whitechapel (immigration trends etc.) It would be more useful to have papers relating to that person's entry/living in Whitechapel, such as rent records.
Cartoons from *Punch* magazine		
Census reports		
Charles Booth's poverty map		
Rent collection record		

5 Why is it difficult for historians to find out about the population of Whitechapel in the late 1800s?

....

....

....

....

....

....

....

....

....

....

....

6 Study Source A carefully. Then look at the statements below. What does the source suggest about the population of Whitechapel?

Source A

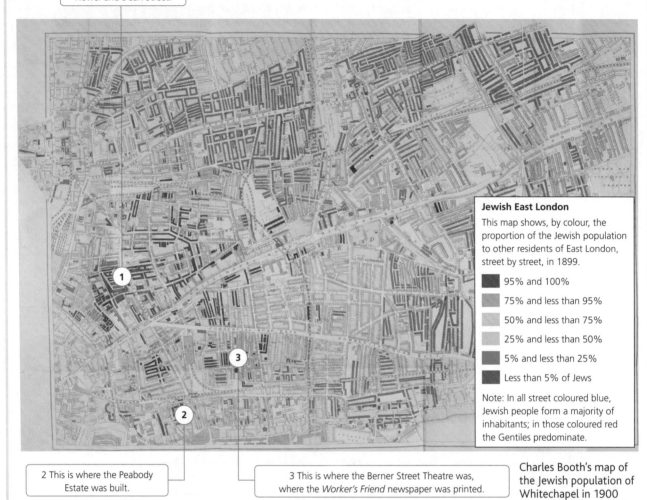

1 This is the area around Flower and Dean Street.

2 This is where the Peabody Estate was built.

3 This is where the Berner Street Theatre was, where the *Worker's Friend* newspaper was printed.

Jewish East London

This map shows, by colour, the proportion of the Jewish population to other residents of East London, street by street, in 1899.

■ 95% and 100%
■ 75% and less than 95%
□ 50% and less than 75%
□ 25% and less than 50%
■ 5% and less than 25%
■ Less than 5% of Jews

Note: In all street coloured blue, Jewish people form a majority of inhabitants; in those coloured red the Gentiles predominate.

Charles Booth's map of the Jewish population of Whitechapel in 1900

	Agree	Disagree
Source A suggests that Whitechapel (and the East End generally) was heavily populated.		
Source A suggests that Jewish people tended to intersperse with other, non-Jewish residents.		
Source A suggests that Jewish settlement spread far across the Whitechapel area and into surrounding areas.		
Source A shows what types of employment Jewish people found in the Whitechapel area.		
Source A demonstrates that certain ethnic groups were concentrated in small areas.		

....

....

....

7 What would it be fair, and sensible, to say after having examined Source A? Try to write a short paragraph that demonstrates what can be learnt from the source.

Source A shows that the population of Whitechapel...

....

....

....

....

8 Below are a number of other sources that could be used to follow up Source A. Place them in order, from the one you think would be the most helpful next step for research (1) to the least helpful (4).

Source	Order (1–4)
Census information for 1901	
Records for a local synagogue in the Whitechapel area	
Memoirs from a resident of the Whitechapel area in 1900	
Plans for slum clearances before the new Peabody Estate was built	

Policing in Whitechapel and the Jack the Ripper case (1888)

9 There is a mistake in each of the sentences below. Identify the mistake and rewrite the sentence with the correct information.

a   A Division was the part of the Metropolitan Police Force that looked after Whitechapel.

....

....

....

b   Edmund Henderson was Metropolitan Police Commissioner during the Jack the Ripper murders of 1888.

....

....

....

c   Autopsy was not yet available to CID detectives during the period of the Whitechapel murders.

....

....

....

d   One of the biggest problems that police in Whitechapel commonly faced during this period was smuggling.

....

....

....

....

....

⑩ What types of source might be useful for finding out more about policing in Whitechapel? An example has been completed for you.

Type of source	Useful or not?	How could it be useful/what could it tell us? or What doesn't it tell us and what could I use instead?
Coroners' reports	Yes	Coroners' reports would give the autopsy findings and circumstances of death. They would record valuable forms of evidence and show us what evidence the police had to go on for their investigations (and how effective the evidence would likely be).
Police sketches of crime scenes and criminals		
National newspaper reports		
Charles Booth's poverty map		
Newspaper cartoons about H Division		

11 Study Source B carefully. Then look at the statements in the table below. What does Source B suggest about policing in Whitechapel?

Source B

A cartoon from the news magazine *Punch*, October 1888 — the posters are advertising newspapers filled with horrible details of the murders

	Agree	Disagree
Source B suggests that the media was interested in the Jack the Ripper case.		
Source B suggests that the police in Whitechapel were not very efficient.		
Source B gives us an impression of what the locality of Whitechapel was like.		
Source B implies that the area of Whitechapel was threatening.		
Source B demonstrates that the police in Whitechapel had a difficult job in the late 1800s.		

12 What would it be fair, and sensible, to say after having looked at Source B? Try to write a short paragraph that demonstrates what can be learnt from the source.

Source B shows that policing in Whitechapel...

....

....

....

....

13 Below are a number of other sources that could be used to follow up source B. Place them in order, from the one you think would be the most helpful next step for research (1) to the least helpful (4).

Source	Order (1–4)
Written newspaper accounts of the Whitechapel murders and investigation in 1888	
The written notes of a police constable from H Division	
An interview with James Monro, the head of CID until 1888	
Court reports involving the Metropolitan Police Force in Whitechapel	

Exam-style questions

Historic environment (Section A)

14 Describe two key features of policing in the Whitechapel area between c.1870 and c.1900.

(6) (4 marks)

- Feature 1:

....

....

....

- Feature 2:

....

....

....

15 a Study Sources C and D. How useful are these sources for an enquiry into housing and accommodation in the Whitechapel area between 1870 and 1900? Explain your answer, using Sources C and D and your own knowledge of the historical context.

(12) (8 marks)

Source C

I have to state that I have made an inspection of all the private houses, or houses let in apartments, in the undermentioned streets, namely — Flower and Dean Street, Upper Keate Street, and Lower Keate Street. The houses, 38 in number, contain 143 rooms, and are occupied by 298 persons; 210 adults and 88 children [...]. I discovered 4 cases of overcrowding only, 2 in Flower and Dean Street, and 2 in Lower Keate Street. The interior condition of these houses is not good, they are worn out, and many of the walls and ceilings are dirty and dilapidated. The greater portion of these houses have been condemned [...], and three of their number, 5, 7, and 8, Lower Keate Street, should either be taken down, or at once closed, as they are in such a dirty and dilapidated condition.

From the Board of Works, Whitechapel district, report on the sanitary condition of the Whitechapel district, for the quarter ended 3 April 1880.